1) Draw a 6... 2) and another 6. 3) Add a big curve to make the body. 4) Add more curvy lines... 5) a question mark... 6) seven sideways wav...

8) and a bunch of woolly, blue 3's!

Doodle a BIGHORN SHEEP

The biggest horns of a bighorn sheep were 50 inches long.

1) Draw an 8.

2) Put a small sideways 8 on top.

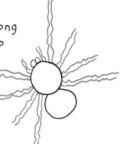

3) Draw eight pairs of long squiggly lines and two pairs of short squiggly lines.

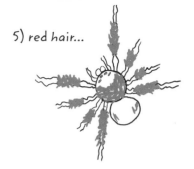

4) Add four tiny 8's...

5) red hair...

6) and black hair— then run!

Doodle a
TARANTULA

Tarantulas not only have 8 legs— they've got 8 eyes, too!

1) Draw a 9.

9

2) Connect top and bottom with a curve.

3) Add two small curves and two teardrops...

4) and a big C.

5) Attach nine curves...

6) then one big curve.

7) Draw three funny-looking 3's.

8) Add two more 3's and a curvy tail...

9) and armor!

Doodle an
ARMADILLO

The nine-banded armadillo wears its favorite number around its middle!

1) Draw two 11's, one taller than the other.

2) Add horizontal lines.

3) Make two big curves across the top...

4) and three descending lines.

5) Add two big curves through the bottom...

6) and lots of cables made of 1's!

Doodle a BRIDGE

The Golden Gate Bridge in San Francisco gets its strength from numbers. It's a suspension bridge held up by cables, and the cables are made of wire—80,000 miles of wire!

1) Draw a 14.

14

2) Make boxes of each number, and add an angle...

3) and two slanted rectangles.

4) Add a line and an arc.

5) Draw another arc and a squashed 0.

6) Draw another arc and another squashed 0.

7) Attach three parallel lines...

8) and another set of three parallel lines.

9) Draw four small curves.

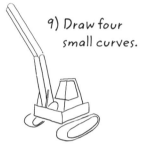

10) Put a 6 on a string and draw three 2's.

11) Add an operator.

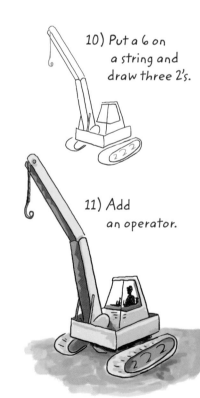

Doodle a
CRANE

Numbers have pull! Cranes use pulleys to pull more weight with less effort. How much less? A single pulley can lift a 100-pound weight with only 50 pounds of force.

1) Write 15.

2) Add a vertical line.

3) Add a trapezoid with fringe.

4) Add a 2 and a 71.

5) Draw a loopy curve and a short line.

6) Add a 17 on top...

7) with a 5 inside to make a hat.

8) Draw five 0's and fringe.

10) Give your snowman a carrot and sticks.

Doodle a SNOWMAN

The biggest snowman in the world was made in 1999 in Maine. This giant Frosty was over 113 feet high, had six tires for his mouth, and two tires for his eyes—but they couldn't find a carrot big enough for his nose. His arms were made of two 10-foot trees.

1) Draw 16 going in two directions.

2) Put a 6 on top.

3) Add curvy lines.

4) Make a little teardrop nose...

5) and add two 10's for eyes.

6) Add lines to make an arm with fingers.

Doodle a LEMUR

Lemurs live only one place on earth—on an island off the coast of Africa called Madagascar.

7) Draw scribble stripes to make a ring-tailed lemur.

 1) Draw a very tall 17.

 2) Add another very tall 17...

 3) and then a 1 on the left and 7 on the right.

4) Connect all of the ends...

5) and make 16,000 windows!

Doodle a
SKYSCRAPER

How would you like a job washing windows at the Sears Tower in Chicago? There are 16,000 windows on 110 floors!

1) Draw two 18's sideways.

2) Connect them with a big rectangle.

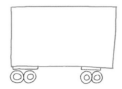

3) Add 47...

5) and connect with lines.

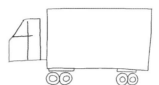

6) Draw a double 0 and perpendicular double lines to make an exhaust pipe.

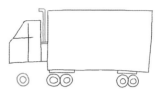

7) Then hop in the driver's seat and start trucking!

Doodle a TRUCK

Big trucks need big numbers to haul big loads! Many have 18 wheels, 10 gears, a 140-gallon fuel tank, and an engine 10 times the size of your family's car. That's so they can carry 8,000-pound loads.

1) Write 19
very slowly.

2) Attach a
curvy line...

3) and big spiral to
make a shell.

4) Add
three small curves...

5) then two vertical lines and
two dot eyes...

7) and a trail of snail slime.

Doodle a
SNAIL

How slow does a snail go? That depends on the snail, of course.
Some speedsters zoom ahead at 55 yards per hour—
but slowpokes plod along at 23 inches per hour!

1) Write 25.

2) Add curves and specks...

3) three 6's...

4) two teardrop ears and two more curves.

5) Attach a big, bean-shaped body.

6) Add four sideways waves and four straight lines for legs...

7) four wedge hooves, a fringe tail, and a beard.

Doodle a
KUDU

The horns on this kudu antelope are longer than its legs—one of the biggest pair ever found measured 61 inches. Imagine running around with your legs on your head!

1) Draw 29.

2) Add another 29.

3) Add some feathers.

4) Draw two curves.

5) Add curvy and straight lines to make two legs.

6) Add more lines to make feet.

Doodle an OSTRICH

Don't challenge the ostrich to a foot race. Ostriches can run 40 mph—but since they weigh over 300 pounds, they can't get off the ground!

1) Draw 32.

2) Attach 37.

3) Add 50 and a slice...

4) a swoopy 6...

5) and connect with a bumpy curve.

6) Add three toes and make your chameleon turn green.

Doodle a CHAMELEON

The three-horned chameleon likes to keep its altitude up. It lives in trees in the high mountains of East Africa.

1) Draw a vertical 34.

2) Put on two 13 shoes.

3) Add a line and two zig-zags...

5) a hat...

6) two arms...

7) and two loopy hands.

Doodle a
DANCER

Tap dancers count with their feet!
They shuffle, step, and stomp to make
the beat—a 1 and a 2 and a 3 and a 4!

1) Write 37.

2) Connect with a 0.

3) Attach a zig-zag line, and draw an 8 and a 0 to form the head.

4) Add a 1 and a 6.

5) Add three 7's.

7) Add four squiggle 7's.

8) Add squiggle feet and wings.

Doodle a PRAYING MANTIS

There are over 1,400 species of praying mantis. The mantis is the only insect that can look over its shoulder. Amen!

1) Draw two
squiggly C's.

2) Add
four angles.

3) Draw four
squiggle legs...

4) four little wedge
hooves...

5) and a squiggle
back and tummy.

6) Add three tears
and an S.

7) Attach the snout so this
little piggy can eat!

Doodle a
PECCARY

Dig this pig! The peccary runs wild in Texas, Mexico, and
South America. Not a fussy eater, it eats fruits, roots,
worms, and lizards.

1) Draw two K's.

2) Add a dotted O and a curlicue.

3) Draw two angles.

4) Make a wave...

5) a straight line, and two Z's.

6) Draw loopy fingers, toes, a squiggle curve...

8) and a hairless tail.

Doodle a QUOKKA

Honey, I shrunk the kangaroo! Quokkas are small kangaroos weighing only 7 pounds. They mostly live on Rottnest Island, near western Australia, where they sleep all day and eat all night.

1) Draw two g's.

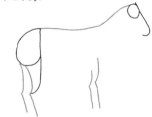

2) Connect with a curve, and make four sideways waves.

3) Draw four lines and wedge hooves.

4) Make a tummy curve.

5) Add a wave, a teardrop ear...

6) fringe tail...

8) squiggle stripes, and a mane.

Doodle a QUAGGA

If you saw a quagga, you might think it had started out as a zebra and then decided to be a horse. But you'll never get a chance to see a living quagga because they were hunted to extinction more than a hundred years ago in South Africa.

1) Draw two Z's.

2) Attach four curves.

3) Draw four ziggy curves.

4) Add two little zigs...

5) ten tiny spots, and two bigger ones.

6) Draw a long, ziggy curve and two ziggy lines...

8) another long, ziggy curve...

9) and ziggy feet!

Doodle a
GRIZZLY

This grizzly bear must have woken up on the wrong side of the bed. Or maybe after sleeping all winter she's just ready for breakfast!

1) Draw two squiggly o's, one on top of the other.

2) Add two L's and two m's.

3) and two more L's.

4) Draw a J...

6) and two squiggle curves.

7) Add a big squiggle curve and a little squiggle curve.

8) Draw squiggle legs and tail...

9) and lots of brown, woolly fur!

Doodle a WOOLLY MAMMOTH

Cold enough for you? Not for the woolly mammoth, which lived during the Ice Age and became extinct more than 12,000 years ago—maybe because the weather had gotten too warm for it to survive. The mammoth's huge tusks were scary looking, but strictly defensive. So what creature would try to attack a woolly mammoth?

1) Draw two b's, one inside the other.

2) Put fringe on top of one and...

3) a curve around the other. Add a big sideways wave.

4) Draw two squiggle lines...

5) add one straight line and a big squiggle curve.

6) Draw a squiggle line and a curve.

7) Add loopy fingers and toes.

12) Make a tree branch to swing from!

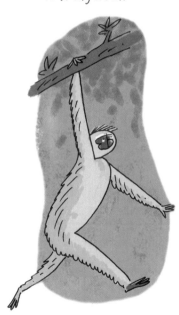

Doodle a
GIBBON

Gibbons are apes that like to move in high places.
They use their very long arms to swing from tree to tree.

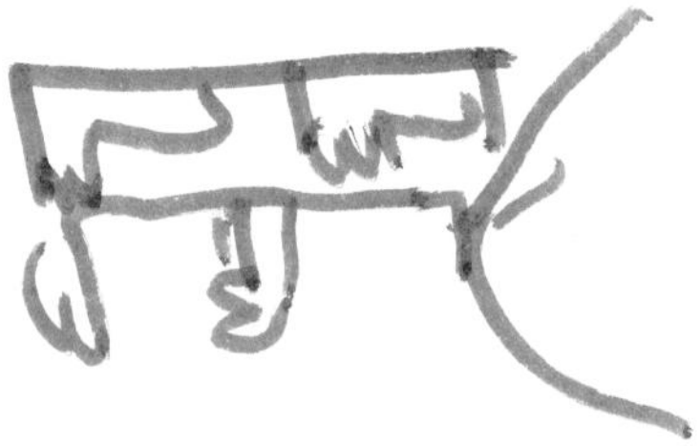

1) Draw tall E's.

2) Add two 2's...and one line...

3) loopy fingers and toes...

4) and two curlicues.

5) Draw a q, p, and e...

6) and a squiggle top.

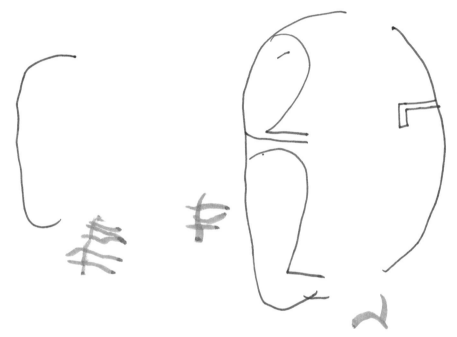

1

7) Give your meerkat whiskers and a large family.

Doodle a MEERKAT

Private Meerkat reporting for guard duty! Meerkats live underground. When they come up to look for food, one meerkat always stands watch.

1) Draw two n's.

2) Add two more n's.

3) Connect with curvy lines.

4) Add four lines...

5) and a U.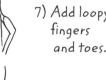

6) Attach four angles.

7) Add loopy fingers and toes...

8) and a curvy S tail.

Doodle a GOANNA

Here's a lizard that can stand on its own two feet! Goannas spend most of their time closer to the ground, but they will stand up to defend themselves.

1) Draw two R's.

2) Add two lines and a little o.

4) Draw a big leaf shape.
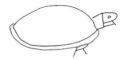

5) Add a big curve.

6) Attach four little L's and a short loop tail.

8) Draw one big zig-zag and three little zig-zags.

9) Add six vertical lines..
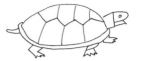

10) and eight curlicues.

Doodle a TERRAPIN

Terrapins are turtles that like it wet—they spend most of their time in water! Diamondback terrapins like it wet and a little salty. They live in low areas on the coast that are flooded each day by ocean tides.

1) Draw two w's.

2) Add three more W's on the left...

3) and two more W's on the right.

4) Connect the W's on the bottom...

5) and on the top.

6) Attach a little c on one end and one more w on the other side.

Doodle a GLOWWORM

These little critters aren't worms and they don't always glow—until they grow up. Glowworms are the larvae of fireflies—which aren't flies and though they light up, they aren't on fire!

7) Add three angles and glow!

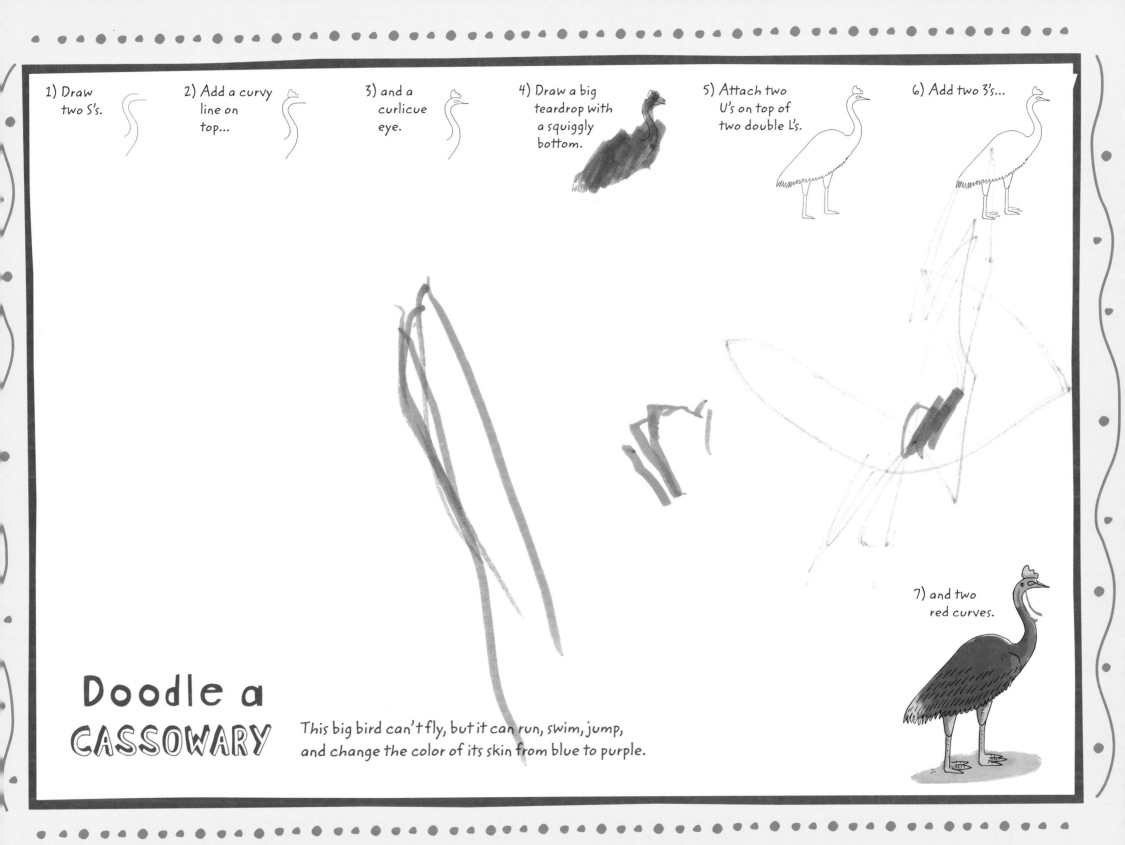

1) Draw two S's.

2) Add a curvy line on top...

3) and a curlicue eye.

4) Draw a big teardrop with a squiggly bottom.

5) Attach two U's on top of two double L's.

6) Add two 3's...

7) and two red curves.

Doodle a CASSOWARY

This big bird can't fly, but it can run, swim, jump, and change the color of its skin from blue to purple.

1) Draw two long curvy sideways L's.

2) Add two curves and a double o eye...

3) and a bean on top.

5) Draw a teardrop body...

6) and two curves.

7) Add loopy wing feathers...

8) and some longer, loopy tail feathers.

9) Draw a loopy claw and a branch to sit on.

Doodle a
HORNBILL

This bird doesn't blow a horn, and that's not a hat on its head. It's a casque—a bony growth that looks like a helmet and gets another wrinkle every year.

1) Draw two o's on a slant.

2) Connect with two l's.

3) Attach two S's.

4) Draw a big teardrop with a squiggle end.

5) Add two bent Y's...

6) a 9 eye...

7) and water!

Doodle a
SPOONBILL

If you invite this bird to dinner, it will bring its own spoon—you just need to serve fish!

1) Draw two cursive i's.

2) Attach two squiggles...

3) and a curve.

4) Draw a sideways W...

5) and connect with a curve.

6) Draw a curvy V beak...

7) and a flower to sip.

Doodle an IIWI

The iiwi is the "double i" state bird of the "double i" state of Hawaii!

1) Draw two little o's.

2) Draw two R's, one on top of the other.

3) Connect with a curve.

4) Add a sideways M...

5) a sideways V...

6) and a sideways W.

7) Draw two little w's and put fringe on top.

Doodle a
KOOKABURRA

This Australian bird is the world's funniest alarm clock.
The kookaburra laughs every day just before sunrise and sunset.

8) Laugh, kookaburra, laugh!

1) Draw
two e's,
one inside
the other.

2) Attach a
curvy
angle.

3) Add a curve
on the bottom...

4) and a curve
on the top.

5) Draw a V
and a Y.

6) Make
loopy feet.

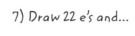

7) Draw 22 e's and...

eeeeeeeeeeeeeeeeeeeeeeeee

Doodle a
REEVE'S
PHEASANT

There's an old song called "Shake a Tail Feather."
For a male Reeve's pheasant, that tail can be
6 feet long!

8) connect them top and bottom.
That's a long ending!

1) Draw two S's.

2) Add two P's.

3) Draw a squiggle...

4) and six curves,

5) and eight short lines.

6) Draw two longer lines...

7) a U on the bottom,

Doodle a GRASSHOPPER

Name that tune! Each species of grasshopper sings a different song. Since there are some 10,000 species, that's a lot of music. Grasshoppers sing by rubbing their legs against their wings. They hear with "ears" in their front legs or abdomens.

8) and a blade of grass.

1) Draw two double line I's.

2) Put an oval through them...

3) and another oval inside that.

4) Add two long, curvy double lines...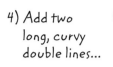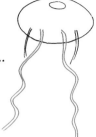

5) and two more...

6) and three more.

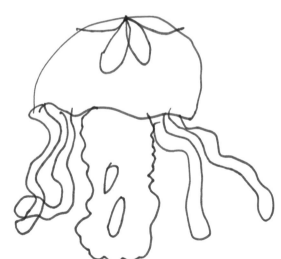

Doodle a
JELLYFISH

Brainless blobs of poisonous tentacles, jellyfish aren't really fish, they're spineless invertebrates.

7) Add some long pink squiggles.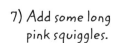